Contents

Some words in the book are in bold, **like this**. You can find out what they mean by looking in the glossary.

Introducing Brazil

Brazil is the largest country in South America. Most people have seen photographs of its vast Amazon rainforests and wonderful beaches. Many have heard of Brazil's famous football players and its fabulous Carnival when thousands of dancers fill the streets. But there is much more to this gigantic country.

Early peoples

People first entered Brazil over 10,000 years ago. Their ancestors almost certainly came from Asia, crossing the frozen Bering Straits into the American continent during the last **Ice Age**. These early people left few artifacts that tell us about their lifestyle. We know most were **nomadic**, hunting and fishing in the forests and rivers. The Tupi-Guarani, one of the larger tribes, occupied land along the coast, the Jê inhabited the centre, and the Arawaks and Caribs were in the north.

The Europeans arrive

The Portuguese explorer, Pedro Álvarez Cabral, landed on the Atlantic coast on 22 April, 1500. Later the country was named Brazil after the brasilwood, a native tree that produces a red dye. The city of Salvador was founded in 1549. It was Brazil's capital until 1763.

The Portuguese explorers discovered that sugar grew well in Brazil's northeast. They forced the native peoples to work for free on **plantations** and also brought in slaves from Africa. The slaves were often treated cruelly and many tried to escape.

Raintree

Marion Morrison

Brazil

Countries Around the World

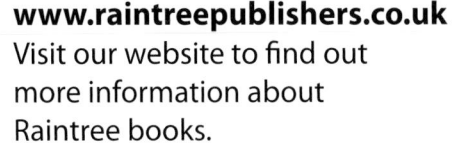
www.raintreepublishers.co.uk
Visit our website to find out more information about Raintree books.

To order:

☎ Phone 0845 6044371
📄 Fax +44 (0) 1865 312263
🖳 Email myorders@raintreepublishers.co.uk

Customers from outside the UK please telephone +44 1865 312262

Raintree is an imprint of Capstone Global Library Limited, a company incorporated in England and Wales having its registered office at 7 Pilgrim Street, London, EC4V 6LB – Registered company number: 6695582

Text © Capstone Global Library Limited 2012
First published in hardback in 2012
First published in paperback in 2013
The moral rights of the proprietor have been asserted.

Edited by Louise Galpine and Megan Cotugno
Designed by Ryan Frieson
Original illustrations © Capstone Global Library, Ltd, 2012
Illustrated by Oxford Designers & Illustrators
Picture research by Tracy Cummins
Originated by Capstone Global Library, Ltd
Printed in China by China Translation and Printing Services

ISBN 978 1 406 22785 7 (hardback)
15 14 13 12 11
10 9 8 7 6 5 4 3 2 1

ISBN 978 1 406 22814 4 (paperback)
16 15 14 13 12
10 9 8 7 6 5 4 3 2 1

British Library Cataloguing in Publication Data
Morrison, Marion.
Brazil. -- (Countries around the world)
981'.065-dc22
A full catalogue record for this book is available from the British Library.

Acknowledgements
We would like to thank the following for permission to reproduce photographs: © Corbis: pp. 30 (© Sylvain Safra/Hemis), 31 (© Julia Waterlow/Eye Ubiquitous); © Getty Images: p. 17 (Luis Veiga); © istockphoto: pp. 19 (© luoman); 33 (© Luciana Bueno Santos); © Photolibrary: pp. 9 (Thomas Kelly), 10 (Luiz C. Marigo), 14 (Anja Kessler), 27 (Florian Kopp); © Shutterstock: pp. 5 (© Celso Diniz), 8 (© Juha Sompinmäki), 13 (© Frontpage), 15 (© Neale Cousland), 20 bottom (© H.Damke), 20 middle (© guentermanaus), 20 top (© Holger Ehlers), 25 (© ostill), 28 (© Jose Miguel Hernandez Leon), 32 (© Celso Pupo), 34 (© gary yim), 38 (© Worldoctopus), 39 (© jbor), 46 (© Atlaspix); © South American Pix: pp. 7, 11 (© Tony Morrison), 23 (© Tony Morrison), 35 (© Bill Leimbach).

Cover photograph reproduced with permission of Photolibrary/Alfio Garozzo.

We would like to thank Luciano Tosta for his invaluable help in the preparation of this book.

Every effort has been made to contact copyright holders of any material reproduced in this book. Any omissions will be rectified in subsequent printings if notice is given to the publisher.

Disclaimer
All the Internet addresses (URLs) given in this book were valid at the time of going to press. However, due to the dynamic nature of the Internet, some addresses may have changed, or sites may have changed or ceased to exist since publication. While the author and publisher regret any inconvenience this may cause readers, no responsibility for any such changes can be accepted by either the author or the publisher.

Rio de Janeiro has some amazing views, including this one of Sugar Loaf Mountain and Botofogo Bay.

History:
an independent nation

The French Emperor Napoleon invaded Portugal in 1807, and the Portuguese royal family fled to Brazil. In 1822 Dom Pedro I, heir to the Portuguese throne, declared Brazil **independent** and himself Emperor. His 14-year-old son Dom Pedro II succeeded him in 1840.

Interested in science and education, Dom Pedro II founded schools, libraries, and academies. Brazil modernized, building railways and roads, a telegraph system, and steamships for transporting the country's main **export**, coffee. **Immigrants** arrived to farm and start businesses, and in 1888 slavery was abolished. But some landowners, army, and church leaders opposed Dom Pedro and he was **deposed** in 1889.

The Republic of Brazil

Brazil became a **republic** with a president as head of state. High demand for rubber from the Amazon brought some wealth, but not for the native peoples. They worked in terrible conditions collecting the rubber **sap** from the trees.

There was little progress for the people until Getúlio Vargas, "The Father of the Poor", was elected president in 1930. He improved living and working conditions. In 1960 President Juscelino Kubitschek **inaugurated** Brasilia as the new capital. He aimed for "fifty years' progress in five."

Military rule

The military seized power in 1964 and governed until 1985. They used "death squads" to kill or torture opponents. The economy improved as industry and manufactured goods replaced coffee as the main export. In the 1980s, mass demonstrations by the people led to new elections. Fernando Collor was elected president in 1990 and Fernando Cardoso from 1995 to 2002. Luiz Inácio Lula da Silva was elected in 2002 after running four times. He was re-elected in 2006.

Dom Pedro II was emperor of Brazil from 1840 to 1889.

Brazilian teenagers love to spend time hanging out with friends.

The percentage of Brazil's ethnic groups

White	Mulatto (mixed white and black)	Black	Other (includes Japanese, Arab, Native Peoples)	Unspecified
53.7%	38.5%	6.2%	0.9%	0.7%

CIA: 2000 census

Who are the Brazilians?

From the 1500s, Brazil's population was made up mostly of Portuguese settlers, Africans, and native peoples. Between 1870 and 1953 about five million immigrants arrived from Italy, Portugal, Spain, Germany, Poland, Russia, the Ukraine, the Middle East, and Japan. Many Japanese settled in São Paulo, which now has the largest Japanese community outside Japan.

About 200 million people now live in Brazil. It is a mixed society. The largest group are descended from immigrants or from marriage between immigrants and native people. The next largest group are *mulattos*, people of mixed immigrant and African descent. The remainder includes a small black population and native people.

Native tribes

Hundreds of thousands of native people were killed or died from diseases after contact with European settlers. Today their numbers are increasing. While most still live in palm-thatched huts, growing a few crops, many have schools, medical centres, and dress in Western clothes. Some, like the Yanomami in the north, and the Kayapo of the Xingú Park, are fighting to defend their land. They are leading protests against mining companies, against plans to build dams on rivers, and against farmers who clear the forests for cattle ranching or crops.

This Kayapo fisherman and his son use bows and arrows to catch fish.

PELÉ (BORN 1940)

Edson Arantes do Nascimento, better known as "Pelé", is a famous Brazilian and one of the greatest football players ever. He first played for Brazil when he was 16, and was a member of three Brazilian teams that won World Cups. He scored 1,281 goals in his career, a world record.

Regions and resources: a land of riches

Brazil is the world's fifth largest country in size and population. It shares borders with ten other countries. It has a coastline over 7,491 kilometres (4,665 miles) long facing the Atlantic Ocean. Most of the country lies between the **Equator** and the **Tropic of Capricorn**. Brazil owns several islands including the island of Fernando do Noronha off the Atlantic coast. It also has some immense rivers. The River Amazon, with around 1,000 **tributaries**, is the largest, while the São Francisco River is the longest river that both begins and ends within Brazil.

This map shows Brazil and its neighbouring countries in South America.

The shopping streets in the Amazon city of Santarem were flooded after storms in June 2009.

Daily life

In 2009 heavy rains hit the north and northeast of Brazil. In areas more used to severe droughts, flood water was roof high. More than 190 towns and cities were affected. Thousands of families, unprepared for such events, lost everything: their homes, their animals, and their way of life.

The regions

The regions of Brazil are very diverse. The far north includes the Guiana highlands and Brazil's highest mountain, the Pico da Neblina at 2,994 metres (9,823 feet). The Brazilian highlands broadly cover the centre of the country while Amazon rainforests extend across much of the north, covering an area almost as large as the United States. The northeast is dry and barren, and suffers frequent droughts. In contrast, the south is rich, green, and heavily **cultivated**. This region is cooler, with occasional frosts in winter and tropical storms that can cause serious flooding.

The Amazon basin

The Amazon **basin**, or Amazonia, is the area in northern South America drained by the Amazon River and its tributaries. Most of Amazonia is in Brazil, but it also extends into eight neighbouring countries.

The source of the River Amazon is in the Andes Mountains of Peru, 161 kilometres (100 miles) from the Pacific Ocean. From its source to its mouth on the Atlantic Ocean, the Amazon flows across the continent for around 6,400 kilometers (4,000 miles). Experts estimate that the river and its tributaries carry about one-fifth of the world's fresh river water. The mouth of the Amazon is large enough to contain an island called Marajó, which is over twice the size of Wales.

Habitats

Amazonia has the largest, and probably the oldest, rainforest in the world, and most of it is in Brazil. The rainforest contains a greater number of plant **species** than any other **habitat** on Earth, with thousands of different species of plants and animals. But Amazonia also contains other habitats, including open **savannah** or grasslands, *cerrado* forests of small twisted trees and grasslands, the **cloud forests** of the Andes to the west, and swampy **mangroves** to the east.

FRANCISCO DE ORELLANA
(1511–1546)

In 1542 the Spaniard Francisco de Orellana and 50 soldiers were the first to make the journey down the Amazon, starting from a small tributary in Ecuador. They survived many dangerous attacks from animals and tribes and completed the journey in about 16 months.

The River Araguaia winds through the Amazon rainforest. Areas on the right bank have been cleared of trees.

Minerals, mining, and a miracle

Brazil has one of the world's largest economies. Its long list of mineral resources includes iron, coal, copper, lead, bauxite, tin, gold, and semi-precious gems such as amethyst and topaz. Carajas in the Amazon is the world's largest iron mine.

Much of Brazil's energy comes from gas and **hydroelectricity**. The Itaipú Dam on the Paraná River is one of the world's largest hydroelectric facilities. In the 1970s, in what became known as "the Brazilian Miracle", the government used these resources to turn Brazil into an industrial nation. Brazil now builds everything from aeroplanes and computers to clothing and shoes. A discovery in 2007 looks set to make Brazil one the world's major producers of oil.

Daily life

Brazilians are great social networkers. More now use mobile phones than landline telephones, and **smart phones** are becoming very popular. About half the population in the cities are online. People who do not have their own computers use cafes and shopping centres where they pay to use the Internet.

These school children work on their Classmate PCs. These are part of a government programme that aims to provide all children in poorer areas with laptops.

The Iguaçu Falls sit on the border between Brazil and Argentina.

Tourism

Brazil's beaches, rainforests, and magnificent scenery are some of its greatest resources. Rio de Janeiro, with Sugar Loaf mountain and the Christ the Redeemer statue overlooking the city, is a must for most visitors, as are the stunning Iguaçu Falls on the border with Argentina. Brazil encourages **eco-tourism** so that tourists can enjoy the country, animals and plants, and the local people without harming the **environment**.

This map shows Brazil's land height and major natural features.

Land height above sea level
- Over 3,000 m (9,843 ft.)
- Over 1,000 m (3,281 ft.)
- Over 500 m (1,640 ft.)
- Over 200 m (656 ft.)
- Below 200 m (656 ft.)

Cultivation and crops

Brazil is the world's largest producer of coffee, and a major producer of sugar and orange juice. Other crops include soya beans, cocoa, cotton, tobacco, corn, and rice. Most large-scale **mechanized** farming is in the south where there is good soil and plenty of rain. In the northeast the soil is poor and the climate very dry. But **irrigation** schemes such as the one around the São Francisco River have made a difference, and this area now produces great quantities of fruit.

Daily life

Brazil **exports** more beef than any other country. In the northeast, cowboys called *vaqueiros* wear leather hats and trousers to protect their legs from the thorny vegetation. In the south, cowboys known as *gaúchos* dress traditionally in flat black hats and baggy trousers. At Centres of *Gaucho* Traditions children learn *gaúcho* dances called *fandangos* – a combination of singing and tap dancing.

Sugar for fuel

Ethanol is a fuel produced from sugarcane. It has been used in Brazil since the 1970s. Now more than 90 per cent of new cars in Brazil can run on ethanol, which costs less than petrol or diesel.

Fishing and forestry

Despite its long coastline and many rivers, Brazil's fishing industry is small. Along the coast, fishermen still use traditional methods and sell their catch locally. But with many valuable woods in the rainforest, forestry is a thriving business. This has resulted in extensive destruction to the Amazon rainforest.

This worker is harvesting coffee beans on a plantation in the state of Minas Gerais.

Brazil's main trading partners

	USA	China	Argentina	Germany	Netherlands
Imports	16.12%	12.61%	8.77%	7.65%	none
Exports	10.5%	12.49%	8.4%	4.05%	5.39%

Wildlife:
a world treasure

Brazil has the largest area of rainforest of any country in the world. Rainforests are made up of different layers – from the forest floor, high up to the **canopy** where trees reach towards the sunlight. Nutrients on the forest floor support and feed the trees. Some, like the Brazil nut and silk cotton trees, are almost 48 metres (150 feet) high. The trees have massive roots, and are covered in mosses, climbing plants, and vines called lianas.

Destruction of the rainforests

The destruction of the rainforest in Brazil began in the 1960s when the government encouraged people to move into the Amazon. Vast areas of the forest were cut or burnt down. The land was cleared to make way for roads, cattle ranching, and mining. Many people are concerned about the effect this has had – not only on animal and plant life, but also on the **environment**.

Why rainforests are important

Rain forests absorb a gas, carbon dioxide, from the air and in turn release oxygen into the air. All forms of life need oxygen. The Amazon rainforests produce more than 20 per cent of the oxygen we breathe. Cutting down the rainforests creates a serious problem. Also, burning the forests sends large amounts of carbon dioxide into the air. Experts believe that this causes the Earth's temperature to warm up. This is known as "global warming".

Amazon cities

There are now many large cities within Brazil's Amazon rainforest. Manaus has a population of about 1.63 million, the port of Belém has 1.4 million, and several cities in the **interior**, such as Porto Velho, have over 230,000 people.

Valuable hardwoods and other trees are cut down when the forest is destroyed.

Top: The stripes on this young tapir will disappear by the time it becomes an adult.

Middle: Pink dolphins live in the Amazon River.

Bottom: Capybaras can purr and bark!

A wealth of wildlife

Brazil's rainforests are massive storehouses of wildlife. They contain about ten per cent of all animal **species** in the world, and about 40,000 plant species. Animals found in the higher levels of the forest include monkeys and colourful birds, such as toucans, macaws, and parrots. Lower down, sloths move slowly through the trees, and anteaters search for food. At the lowest level of the forest, there are insects, frogs, and reptiles, including some of the world's largest snakes.

Larger mammals include the jaguar and puma (cougar). The tapir, weighing up to 300 kilograms (700 pounds) is the heaviest animal found in the Amazon forests. The capybara is the largest **rodent**. Rivers in Amazonia are full of life, including electric eels and piranha fish, which can be dangerous.

Endangered species

The destruction of the rainforest has threatened the habitats of many species, while some animals have been deliberately hunted for their skins. Jaguars are listed as threatened. The giant otter, the beautiful purple hyacinth macaw, and the harpy eagle are endangered. Some small marmosets are also considered threatened.

New discoveries

Even today, new species are discovered in the Amazon rainforest. One of the most recent is a type of monkey called Mura's saddleback tamarin. It is named after a local tribe, the Mura. It is only 24 centimetres (9.4 inches) tall, but has a **prehensile** tail about 32 centimetres (12.6 inches) long, which it uses to hang from trees.

Saving the environment

Brazil has almost 60 national parks and many reserves that protect animals, plants, and landscapes. Near Brasilia, the Emas National Park is a grassland home to the giant anteater, the maned wolf, and the ostrich-like greater rhea. The Lençóis Maranhenses National Park in the northeast protects sand dunes and lagoons. In the southwest, the Pantanal National Park is a tropical wetland with several endangered species, including the marsh deer, the hyacinth macaw, and the jaguar.

Daily life

The rainforest contains many plants with medical properties that native peoples have used for centuries. Many Brazilians prefer them to ordinary medicine. Quinine from the cinchona tree is used to fight malaria. Curare – a poison that native tribes use to stun animals – relaxes muscles. Scientists believe that many more such plants have yet to be discovered.

Mata Atlântica

The Atlantic rainforest, known as the Mata Atlântica, once grew along the Brazilian coast. Today, more than 90 per cent has disappeared. In cities such as Rio de Janeiro and São Paulo, roads, industry, and farming have helped to destroy this rainforest. Even so, scientists have recorded numerous species there of which a third are found nowhere else on Earth. Because of its importance, some of the remaining Mata Atlântica is now being protected.

Golden lion tamarin

With the destruction of the Mata Atlântica, the golden lion tamarin almost became extinct. Fortunately, scientists were able to take a few into captivity. They bred, and were later introduced into the wild. Some appear to have survived, but are still in danger.

Herbal medicines are on sale in the main square of Guajaramerim, an Amazon town.

Infrastructure:
a democratic country

Brazil is a **republic** governed by a president and a congress. The president
is elected for four years and can be re-elected for a further four years. The
congress is made up of the Senate with 81 senators elected for eight years
and the Chamber of Deputies with 513 deputies elected for four years.
Members can be re-elected any number of times. Congress makes the laws
and there are courts to make sure the laws are followed. The Supreme Federal
Tribunal is the most important court.

Key
- Agriculture
- Mines and deposits
- Country borders

This map shows agricultural and mining
areas of Brazil.

Brazil is divided into 26 states and the Federal District of Brasilia. Each state elects its own governor and council, and has districts that elect mayors and councils. People can vote from the age of 16, and must vote between 18 to 70 years old.

Brasilia

Brasilia replaced Rio de Janeiro as the capital city in 1960. It was built from scratch and designed by the famous architects Oscar Neimeyer and Lucio Costa. Some say it is the shape of an aeroplane, others that it is based on the shape of a bow and arrow. Most of the government buildings are at the point where the arrow crosses the bow.

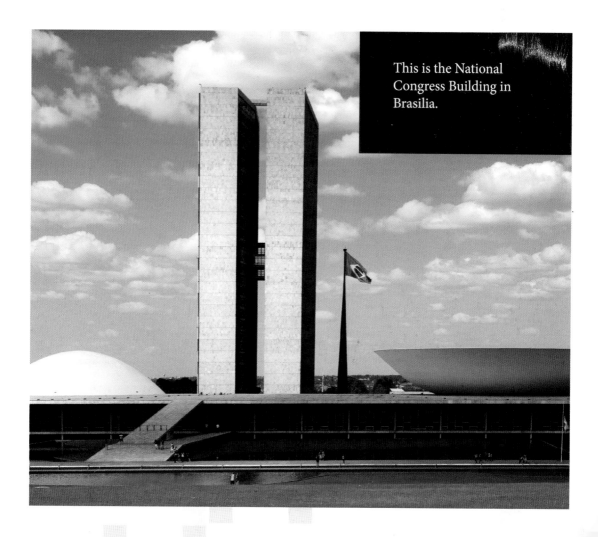

This is the National Congress Building in Brasilia.

Getting an education

School in Brazil is similar to school in the United Kingdom. There are state and private schools. Pupils study subjects such as languages, history, geography, science, art, and sports. Their uniforms are usually white T-shirts with coloured trousers or skirts. However, many schools, especially in rural areas, are short of equipment and teachers. Even in towns, pupils often go to school in shifts – some in the morning and others in the afternoon – because the schools cannot manage them all at the same time.

Working children

The children of poorer families often leave school to go to work. Since the 1990s, the government has helped these poor families, so their children can stay at school. So far the scheme has been successful. The number of working children aged between 5 and 14 fell by more than 50 per cent between 1992 and 2008. There are also some special schools for children, often orphans, who work on the street selling trinkets or cleaning cars. However, 14 million children and teenagers still do not attend school in Brazil. Over 10 per cent of people over 15 years old cannot read or write.

The Brazilian population by age groups

0–14 years	15–64 years	65 years and over
26.7%	66.8%	6.4%

CIA: est. 2010

How to say...

Portuguese is Brazil's official and most widely spoken language. Spanish, German, Italian, English, and Japanese are also in use. There are also many native languages. A typical Portuguese phrase is *"Como é que eu chego lá?"* (Ko-mo e ke e-oo she-go laa?), which means "How do I get there?"

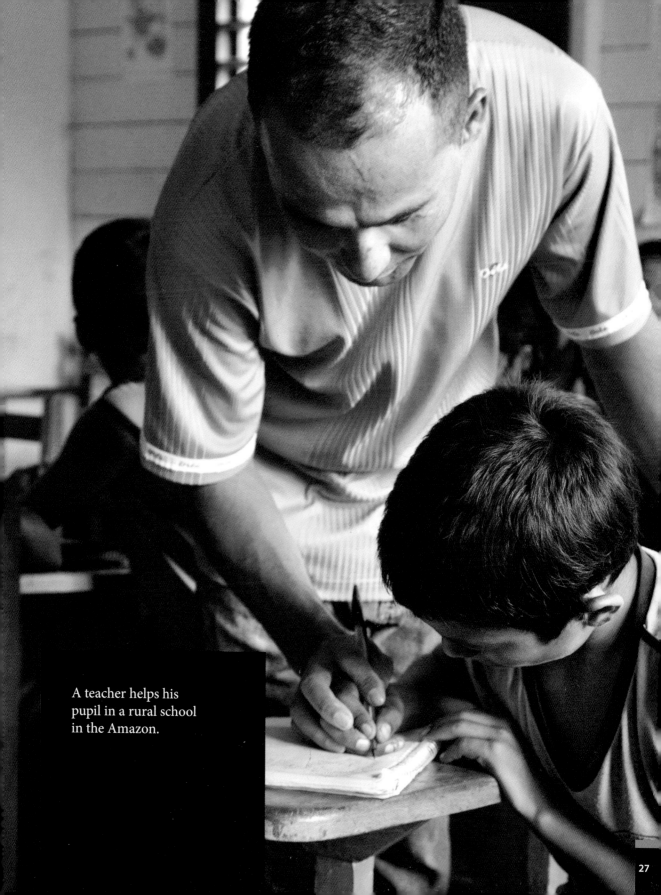

A teacher helps his pupil in a rural school in the Amazon.

Living in Brazil

In Brazil there is a big gap between the rich and the poor. Some of the poorest families earn less than £25 per month. In 2003 President Lula formed the *Bolsa Familia*, a government programme that gives money to poorer families. It benefits 12 million families. There has already been a drop in the level of poverty.

City dwellers

About 86 per cent of Brazilians live in towns or cities. Millions moved from rural areas hoping for better education and medical care. But many have not found work and cannot afford housing. Instead they live in **favelas** – slums or shantytowns – which often sit alongside nice houses where wealthier people live. Some favelas are very dangerous places because of drugs and violence. There are social organizations that work to help the children of the favelas.

One of Rio de Janeiro's largest favelas covers a hillside next to modern highrise apartments.

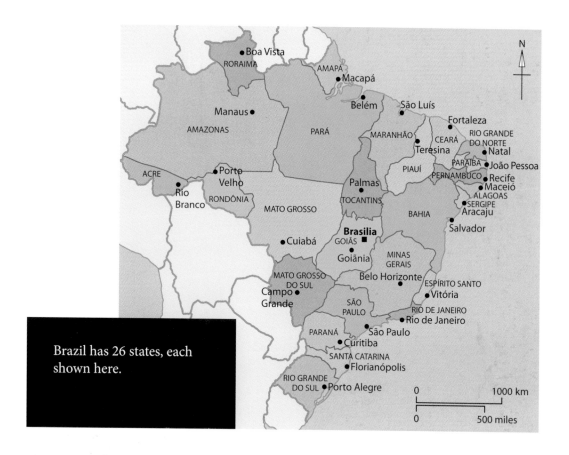

Brazil has 26 states, each shown here.

Daily life

São Paulo is the largest city in South America. The population of nearly 130,000 in 1893 has grown to about 20 million today. The city is the industrial, commercial, and transport centre of the country. The streets are jammed with traffic, which, together with industry, has caused severe air pollution, leaving the city often covered by dull grey smog.

Staying healthy

Staying healthy is difficult if you do not have clean water or enough food. In 2000 Brazil was ranked 125th on a world health list. But children do get vaccinations against most diseases, and the standard of health has been improving. More children under five are surviving. Life expectancy – the length of time a person is expected to live – has increased.

Culture:
Brazilians at play

Brazilians love music – they love to play, dance, and sing. Their music and instruments owe much to African traditions. An example is the samba, which is the music and dance most associated with Brazil. A martial arts-style dance that also has African origins is the high-kicking *Capoeira*. Heitor Villa-Lobos is Brazil's most famous classical musician and composer.

Arts and literature

Brazil has internationally famous artists, sculptors, architects, writers and filmmakers. The 20th century artist Cândido Portinari painted **murals** with social themes and some can be seen in the **United Nations** building in New York. Oscar Neimeyer and Lucio Costa were the designers of Brasilia. Jorge Amado, the writer, used his own upbringing in northeast Brazil in many of his novels.

These drummers are part of an Afro-Brazilian music group that are performing in Carnival in Salvador de Bahia.

This soapstone sculpture of the prophet Oseas was sculpted by O Aleijadinho. It stands outside the Church Bom Jesus do Matozinho in Congonhas.

"O ALEIJADINHO" (AROUND 1738–1814)

Born around 1738, Antõnio Francisco Lisboa is better known as *"O Aleijadinho"* or "The Little Cripple". Although disabled, he became one of Brazil's most famous artists, creating sculptures while lying on his side and his back. His best works, including a church he designed, built, and decorated, are in the old towns of the state of Minas Gerais.

Brazilian filmmakers, such as Walter Salles, Jr, and Fernando Meirelles, have won international awards with films such as *Central Station*, the story of a young boy who makes friends with a teacher, and *City of God*, about two boys from a **favela**. Brazil's most famous actress – although she was born in Portugal – was Carmen Miranda, who was a huge success in Hollywood in the 1940s and 1950s. Gisele Bündchen, from southern Brazil, is a world famous model.

This crowded Copacabana beach is in Rio de Janeiro.

YOUNG PEOPLE

Many young people in Rio take part in *favela* painting projects. Now some of the hillside shacks are painted in rainbow colours and have large murals on the walls.

Food and fun

Food varies across the different regions of Brazil, but almost everywhere people eat *feijoada*, the national dish of rice, smoked meats, and black beans. People of the northeast cook African-style food with coconut, nuts, oils, and fish. In the south, with its large cattle ranches, beef is popular. In Amazonia, among the native peoples, *mandioca*, a vegetable with large roots, is grated and made into a form of bread.

Brazilians at play

At weekends Brazilians crowd on to beaches to sunbathe, play games, and keep fit. Brazilians are passionate about sports, especially football, and the national team have won the World Cup a record five times. When they win an important match, work stops, and everyone fills the streets waving flags, and honking car horns to celebrate. Brazilians are also successful in many other sports, including Formula 1 car racing. Brazil has had three world champions.

Feijoada

This dish is enjoyed by many Brazilians. Ask and adult to help you make it.

Ingredients

- 340 grams jerked (dried) beef
- 450 grams smoked pork
- 450 grams smoked tongue
- 112 grams bacon
- 450 grams smoked sliced sausage
- 1 pig's foot (hock)
- 185 grams black beans
- 1 chopped onion
- 1 chopped fresh sausage
- 1 chopped garlic clove
- dash of cayenne pepper
- 1 chopped shallot

Method

Soak beans and beef overnight in cold water. Drain beef, cover with cold water, bring to boil and boil for 15 minutes. Drain again and cool. Add all the meats, cover with warm water, bring slowly to boil and simmer until tender. In another pot place drained beans, cover with cold water and boil until almost tender. Combine the two pots and simmer until tender. Meanwhile fry the onion and sausage until lightly browned, then add garlic and pepper. Add one cup of cooked beans, mix well and mash together. Stir in some bean-cooking liquid and simmer for 5 to 10 minutes. Return this sauce to the beans and meats and simmer until well blended.

To serve: Separate meats on to one dish, the beans in a hot tureen, and serve with a bowl of rice and slices of orange.

Brazil today

From its many different roots, Brazil has become an increasingly successful nation. Differences in background and belief combine to form a uniquely Brazilian society. For example, Brazil has more Catholics than any country in the world, but many Brazilians are today changing to **evangelical** faiths. Large numbers of Brazilians also follow African religions, such as *Umbanda* and *Candomblé*. Followers hope to find solutions to their problems by making contact with a spirit in another world through a **medium**.

"The greatest show on Earth"

Every year, 40 days before Easter, Carnival takes place in many Brazilian cities. The parade in Rio de Janeiro has religious origins, but today it is a competition between "samba schools." Most samba schools come from the city's poorer neighbourhoods. Each school has a theme, composes music, and designs fantastic costumes and floats. With about 4,000 dancers in each school, it takes a year to prepare.

Every year dancers wear amazing costumes at Rio de Janeiro Carnival.

Looking to the future

Brazil is a country with everything going for it. It has a strong and growing economy, stable government, a young population, and the resources to tackle its major problems of poverty and pollution. It will host the 2014 football World Cup and the 2016 Olympic Games. It will be the first time a South American country has hosted the Olympics. On hearing the news, President Lula summed up the feelings of many Brazilians when he said that "the world has recognized that the time has come for Brazil".

Followers of Umbanda celebrate the festival of Iemanja, the goddess of the sea.

Fact file

Country name: Federative Republic of Brazil

Capital: Brasilia

Language: Portuguese, Spanish, native languages

Religion: Roman Catholic, Afro-Brazilian religions, Evangelical

Type of government: Federal Republic

Independence date: 7 September 1822

National anthem: "Hino Nacional Brasileiro"
*The placid banks of Ipiranga
heard the resounding cry of a heroic people
and in shining rays, the sun of liberty
shone in our homeland's skies at this very moment.*

*If the assurance of this equality
we achieved by our mighty arms,
in thy bosom, O freedom,
our chest shall defy death itself!*

*O beloved,
idolized homeland,
Hail, hail!*

Population: 198,739,269 (est. 2010)

Life expectancy: total population: 71.99 years; male: 68.43 years; female: 75.73 years (est. 2010)

Bordering countries: French Guiana, Suriname, Guyana, Venezuela, Colombia, Peru, Bolivia, Argentina, Paraguay, Uruguay

Total land area: 8,514,877 square kilometres (3,287,612 square miles)

Largest cities: São Paulo (population 11,037,593)
Rio de Janeiro (population 6,186,710)
Salvador (population 2,998,056)
Brasilia (population 2,606,885)

Climate: mostly tropical, but temperate in the south

Major landforms: mostly flat to rolling lowlands in north; some plains, hills, mountains, and narrow coastal belt

Major rivers: Amazon, Madeira, Paraguay, São Francisco

Highest elevation: Pico da Neblina – 2,994 metres (9,823 feet)

Lowest elevation: sea level – 0 metres (0 feet)

Coastline: 7,491 kilometres (4,665 miles)

Currency: Real

Resources: bauxite, gold, iron ore, manganese, nickel, phosphates, platinum, tin, uranium, petroleum, hydropower, timber

Industries: textiles, shoes, chemicals, cement, lumber, iron ore, tin, steel, aircraft, motor vehicles other machinery

Agricultural products: coffee, soya beans, wheat, rice, corn, sugarcane, cocoa, citrus fruit, beef

Imports: machinery, electrical and transport equipment, chemical products, oil, automotive parts, electronics

Exports: transport equipment, iron ore, soya beans, footwear, coffee, cars

National holidays:

1 January	New Year's Day
February/March	Carnival
March/April	Good Friday and Easter Sunday
21 April	Tiradentes Day (honouring a local hero)
1 May	Labour Day
June	Corpus Christi
7 September	Independence Day
12 October	Our Lady of Aparecida (patron saint of Brazil)
2 November	All Souls Day (Day of the Dead)
15 November	Proclamation of the Republic
25 December	Christmas Day

Famous Brazilians:

Jorge Amado (1912–2001), writer
Gisele Bûndchen (born 1980), model and actress
Lucio Costa (1902–1998), architect

The statue of Christ the Redeemer overlooks Sugar Loaf mountain in Rio de Janeiro.

Juscelino Kubitschek (1902–1976),
  president and founder of Brasilia
Antônio Francisco Lisboa ("Aleijadinho")
  (around 1738–1814), sculptor
Luiz Inácio Lula da Silva (born 1945), president 2003–2010
Fernando Meirelles (born 1955), film director
Carmen Miranda (1909–1955),
  actress and samba singer
Ronaldo Luis Nazário de Lima (born 1976), football player
Oscar Niemeyer (born 1907), architect
Cândido Portinari (1903–1962), artist
Walter Salles Jr (born 1956),
  film director and screenwriter
Ayrton Senna (1960–1994),
  world champion racing driver
Edson Arantes do Nascimento ("Pelé")
  (born 1940), football player
Heitor Villa-Lobos (1887–1959),
  classical musician and composer

São Paulo is the largest city in
South America.

Timeline

BC is short for "before Christ". BC is added after a date and means that the date occurred before the birth of Jesus Christ, for example, 450 BC.

c. 13,000–8000 BC	First people arrive in Brazil
c. 8000–1500 BC	Land occupied by nomadic hunting and fishing tribes
1500	Portuguese explorer Pedro Álvarez Cabral lands in Brazil
1549	Salvador de Bahia is established and becomes the capital until 1963
1554	Priests establish a mission at São Paulo
1565	Rio de Janeiro is established
1695	Bandeirantes find gold in Minas Gerais
1763	Rio de Janeiro becomes capital of Brazil
1808	Portuguese royal family are **exiled** to Brazil
1822	Brazil declares **independence** with Dom Pedro I as Emperor
1825	Independence is recognized by Portugal
1840	Emperor Dom Pedro II is crowned
1888	Law to abolish slavery is passed
1889	Emperor Dom Pedro II is deposed and Brazil becomes a Republic
1870–1934	Over 5 million immigrants settle in Brazil

1930–1945	Getúlio Vargas is president
1956	Juscelino Kubitschek becomes president
1960	Brasilia is inaugurated as the new capital city
1964	The start of 21 years of **military dictatorship**
1985	Democratic government is restored
1992	Fernando Collor de Mello, first president to be elected after military regime, removed due to **corruption**
1994	Fernando Henrique Cardoso elected president; re-elected in 1998
2003	Luis Início Lula de Silva elected president; re-elected in 2006
2010	Elections take place with Dilma Rousseff elected as the first female president of Brazil

Glossary

basin large area that is drained by a river and its tributaries

canopy leafy branches at the top of the rainforest

cerrado Brazilian name for an area of grassland and low trees

cloud forest forest at high altitude that is permanently covered in cloud

corruption loss of order or obedience in an organization

cultivate farming the land to produce crops

depose remove someone from a position of authority

eco-tourism responsible travel that protects the environment, animals, and plants, and benefits local people

environment natural world

Equator imaginary circle around the Earth which is the same distance from the north and south poles

ethanol fuel produced from sugarcane

evangelical describes protestant churches that base their teaching on the gospel

exile to force a person or people to move away

export goods and services sold by a country to other countries

favela slum in Brazilian cities

gaúcho cowboy of the southern grasslands of Brazil

habitat natural home of plants and animals

hydroelectricity electricity derived from the movement of water

Ice Age time in the distant past when a large portion of the Earth was covered in ice

immigrant person who moves from one country to another to live there

import goods and services bought by a country from other countries

inaugurate start or open a building or public service with an official ceremony

independent when a country is governed by its own people

interior part of a country distant from the coast

irrigation use of water to help plants to grow

mangrove tree with stilt-like roots that grows in salty shallow water areas in tropical countries

mechanized using machinery or vehicles

medium someone who claims to be able to communicate with spirits or the dead

military dictatorship form of government where all power rests with the armed forces

mural wall painting

nomadic lifestyle of regularly moving from one place to another

plantation large area of land where crops usually of the same type are grown

prehensile something adapted for wrapping around an object

republic independent country whose head of government is not a king or queen

rodent group of mammals that include mice, rats, and guinea pigs

sap milky liquid found in plants

savannah grassland dotted with trees

smart phone mobile phone with Internet connection

species particular type of animal or plant

tributary river or stream that flows into a larger river or stream

Tropic of Capricorn imaginary line circling the Earth south of the Equator at a latitude of 23.27 degrees

United Nations international organization that promotes peace, security, and co-operation

vaqueiro cowboy of the northeast region of Brazil

Find out more

Books

Brazil (Destination Detectives), Ali Brownlie Bojang (Raintree (2007)

Brazil (Discover Countries), Edward Parker (PowerKids Press, 2010)

Brazil (Fact Finders), Brandy Bauer (Capstone, 2007)

Brazil (National Geographic Countries of the World), Zilah Deckker (National Geographic, 2008)

Brazil (The Changing Face Of), Edward Parker (Wayland, 2007)

The Vanishing Rainforest, Richard Platt (Frances Lincoln, 2006)

Websites

www.kidscornerbrazil.org
Go on a virtual journey to Brazil!

kids.nationalgeographic.com/kids/places/find/brazil
Country facts, information, photos and videos about Brazil can be found here.

www.bbc.co.uk/scotland/education/geog/population/case_brazil.shtml
Find out more about everyday life in Brazil on this website.

www.britannica.com/bps/search?query=brazil
Learn more about Brazil from the Encyclopaedia Britannica.

Places to visit

If you are ever lucky enough to travel to Brazil, here are some fascinating places you can visit:

Iguaçu Falls

www.southamericanpictures.com/collections/iguazu/iguazu.htm

Sugar Loaf Mountain, Rio de Janeiro

www.braziltravelvacation.com/sugar-loaf-mountain.html

Christ the Redeemer on Corcovado mountain, Rio de Janeiro

www.braziltravelvacation.com/christ-redeemer.html

Brasilia

www.braziltravelvacation.com/brasilia.html

Topic tools

You can use these topic tools for your school projects. Trace the map onto a sheet of paper, using the thick black outlines to guide you.

The Brazilian flag is green with a dark blue globe in the centre on a large yellow diamond. The globe bears 27 stars representing the states of Brazil, and a white band with the words *Ordem e Progresso* – Order and Progress. Copy the flag design and then colour in your picture. Make sure you use the right colours!

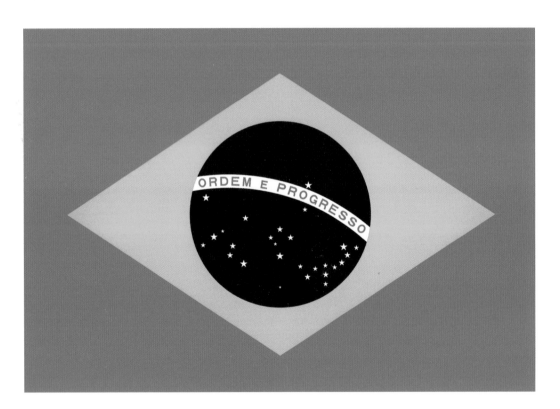

N

Brasilia ■

Index